I AM
Perfect
FOR THIS

Reflections for Entrepreneurs

DR. KATHLEEN T. LENOVER

I am Perfect for This: Reflections for Entrepreneurs
Published by Education for Abundant Living
By Dr. Kathleen T. Lenover
Denver, CO

ISBN: 9798850530488
BUSINESS & ECONOMICS / Entrepreneurship

Cover and Interior design by Victoria Wolf,
wolfdesignandmarketing.com.

QUANTITY PURCHASES: Schools, companies, professional
groups, clubs, and other organizations may qualify for special
terms when ordering quantities of this title.

CONTENTS

I AM PERFECT FOR THIS

Kathleen's Legacy

THE LIFE OF Doctor Kathleen Lenover was one of sacred service, world travel, dancing and a powerful commitment to her family and beloved community of friends. She believed in pursuing spiritual sanctuary while embracing joy as a life choice. She dreamed of writing a series of books, dedicated to supporting the spiritual and entrepreneurial elements of the journeys of all who knew her or perhaps wished they did.

Kathleen transitioned to a higher plane on August 14, 2020, just one day after finishing the final draft of this book's manuscript. A small group of editors, designers and friends brought her book—this book—to publication, honoring her wish to be a published author and, more than that, honoring her intention to inspire entrepreneurs by sharing her own unique and powerful stories.

Kathleen's was a life lived through conscious choices, whether moving from her vow of poverty to a life of prosperity or from the love of a specific religion to embracing all the world's spiritual traditions. Throughout her life she chose conscious connections. She chose to let her light shine brightly and to be a luminary. She chose love.

In love, we humbly share with you this one glorious piece of her extraordinary legacy.

— Rev. Dr. David S. Goldberg, *Editor*
— Julie Mierau, *Co-Editor*

INTRODUCTION

THEY SAY WE DIE TWICE —once when we physically succumb to death and again when people stop telling our stories. Writing elongates the time of our effectiveness, relevance, and ability to make a difference.

Frankly, writing is part of my legacy. Oprah and Deepak, in their meditation series, share that our true legacy is composed of every interaction we have, each experience of love, and every instance of reaching out. Cumulatively, I have come to realize my life story is blessed with unusual experiences, an intense desire for personal growth, and a hunger to make a positive difference. I need to write. I write for you.

Yes, we write what we know. I am intimately

familiar with being a deeply spiritual, professional, entrepreneurial woman with a history of unlearning and relearning new directions for life. Thus, the focus in this literary piece is to invite you to reflect. I want you to receive information that will have your head nodding or being still in that reflective response when you know you are in the presence of something important.

At the end of each chapter I gently ask you to think and feel even more and to act. Questions, suggestions, and references will enrich your experience of deeply examining your life.

A beloved friend and mentor, Dr. Kenn Gordon, advised me to imagine a person to be the object of my wisdom. I would like you to meet my fictional composite of many real-life travelers I call friends. See if you can identify with any or all of them.

Meet Claudia. She felt incredibly frustrated yet exhilarated, realizing that her small voice would be given the audience it deserved. "I get ideas, suppress them, then watch them rear their heads again. I play this game until I know it is repeating itself enough to say 'there's value here' and I should pay attention."

Curious, I inquired, "Which idea is emerging now?"

Frustration and overwhelm quivered in her voice as she shared, "I think I want to quit my government job and start massage school. But I just turned 51. I enjoy a guaranteed income and my family needs that. My benefits are awesome, and I love the folks I work with. Nagging questions emerge. Will I enjoy being on my own? What if I find massage work too hard physically and I hate it? Is this too risky? I'm scared."

At that point I realized the courageous leap Claudia faced. She needed to surround herself with experienced entrepreneurs, knowledgeable financial folks, and positive coaches. She felt like she was jumping from the frying pan into the fire. I knew I needed to write a guidebook to help Claudia with her deliberations.

Welcome to *I Am Perfect for This: Reflections for Entrepreneurs*. The internet is flooded with practical ideas on how to access capital, market yourself, and build a sustainable business you love. Herein you will find many practical gems that you will be blessed knowing.

Yet, this work goes beyond that. This is the reflective dive into the inner workings of the brave souls willing to reach for their dreams.

Thank you for exploring the practical—and deeply spiritual—side of making life changes with ease and grace.

I recently bought a sweatshirt that reads, "This Is Just What I Do. I Drink Wine. I Ballroom Dance. And I Know Things." This book is meant to share with you some of the things I know. The wine and dancing are up to you!

ABOUT THE AUTHOR

DR. KATHLEEN LENOVER, MEd, CFP, MCS, CFC, brought a unique combination of skill sets: 13 years teaching as a Catholic Sister, 33 years a financial advisor, more than 57 years as a licensed/ordained spiritual leader. All of this assisted her in bringing compassion and understanding as client's experience being truly heard and supported.

She was founding minister of Education for Abundant Living, an approved ministry in Centers for Spiritual Living and an acknowledged organization within the New Thought Movement. Dr. Kathleen has been featured on the ABC Home Show, CBS Morning Show, National Public Radio, and was a columnist for *Science of*

Mind Magazine. She was author of a white paper, *What Women Want*, a contributor to Cynthia James' book, *I Choose Me*, and authored a forward to the cutting-edge book on investing, *The Wealth Solution, Bringing Structure to Your Financial Life*.

Dr. Kathleen resided in Denver CO.

DEDICATION

THIS BOOK IS LOVINGLY dedicated to the Sisters of Charity of Cincinnati, acknowledging their unwavering faith and support of me from grade school through college years and beyond. Having the opportunity to live with, be a colleague to, and be called Sister within a phenomenal group of powerfully spiritual women has been a privilege. For those individual Sisters with whom I lived while on mission, as well as the lifelong deep relationships among those who call themselves "Formers," I am humbly grateful.

For all that has been, THANKS.
For all that will be, YES!
— Dag Hammarskjöld

FOREWORD

DEAR FELLOW SEEKERS:

I have always loved Dr. Howard Thurman's statement, "Don't ask what the world needs. Ask what makes you come alive, and go do it. Because what the world needs is people who have come alive."

Kathleen Lenover, with her many years of experience in the corporate and spiritual worlds, mastered what many never seem to realize: an intentional person needs the balance of both. After joining the Sisters of Charity in Cincinnati, Ohio, and teaching in urban schools, Kathleen's work and consciousness expanded as she became a financial planner. Her formal education, combined with decades of practical experience, helped clients, customers, and congregants create and maintain prosperity and abundance in their lives by applying spiritual principles to money management.

Kathleen, as the "Minister of Finance," was a unique and powerful voice on financial matters and money as a prosperity columnist in *Science of Mind* magazine. And her "Monday's Money" video vignettes on social media reached thousands of people around the globe.

It is one thing to be a visionary seeking expression as an entrepreneur. It is something altogether different to allow your dream to continue to unfold and grow with the times. There is truly a sacred understanding as to why some reach their dreams and some do not—storytelling.

Storytelling, aside from being the heartbeat of someone we love, is nature's most ancient method of aligning us with our inner determination. Since the beginning of time—whether through the spoken word, drawings, or art—we have been healed and revealed through our stories.

This book will awaken within you what you have been allowing to sleep. As you read each story, you will have more than an "ah-ha" moment; you will shift into your innate self, an intentional spirit. Intentional people as entrepreneurs are different than people with goals and vision boards. The individuals who align with their vision do not allow outside circumstances, problems, and societal limitations to keep them from realizing their dreams.

Why is this book by Kathleen Lenover so necessary? She is doing more than writing a book. She is a proven success and the stories she represents in her new book, *I Am Perfect for This: Reflections for Entrepreneurs* are each designed to ignite a fire within you.

When visionaries miss their fire, when their passions are tested, it is easy for them to either attempt to be like someone else, copy what another company or person did, project onto others, or live in the need to be right. The vision begins to fade because people focus on the corporate side of success and leave the spiritual guidance at the door.

Authentic lasting success is interwoven with happiness. Such success comes from knowing you did not get where you are by yourself. And one of the greatest celebrations is watching all the people on your team come alive simply because you have.

This book allows you to not only see beyond

your five senses and your common sense but also encourages you to lead with intuition, perception, and insight.

Whether you are living your dreams or they are yet to unfold, you are perfect for this! Kathleen Lenover's beautiful stories will change your career trajectory as they will change you.

Remember, you are not waiting on your dreams to come true. Your dreams are waiting on you to come through. *I Am Perfect for This: Reflections for Entrepreneurs* is just like Kathleen Lenover—original, essential, and necessary.

TEMPLE HAYES

Spiritual Leader, Author, Difference Maker and Founder of The Institute for Leadership and Lifelong Learning, International, www.illli.org

CHAPTER ONE

Find Your Next Adventure

SO MANY OF US became crystal clear about what our expertise is from previous careers where we learned to be efficient, competent, and influential. As we evolve to a new field in our lives, old doubts, some even from childhood, rear their ugly heads, messing with our minds, our self-confidence, and our potential effectiveness. Realizing what a gift we are and honoring our passion for the new adventure is a crucial step in the development of our own self-confidence.

OLD STORIES

Traveling into adulthood we inadvertently carry old programs from our childhood's impressionable years. Our opportunity now is to ask the most powerful question: Does it serve me today?

I no longer take all my parents' and teachers' opinions as gospel. I co-create my reality. If the story serves me, I maintain it. If not, I silently say, "Cancel, cancel."

The transformational power of this "cancel-cancel" technique vividly presented itself during a school incident. I was on staff in an urban-core junior high school where the kids were diverse and incredibly blessed.

They had a principal willing to trust the faculty to provide alternative behaviors for urban survival. Unique skills were taught straight from the curriculum of Silva Mind Control: mindfulness, meditation, deep breathing, controlling our thoughts, and a discipline around how our life stories are told. My heart sang as I watched the teens become proficient at this.

It was a crisp, dry typical Colorado fall day, and the buzz of anticipation rose as we approached the three o'clock dismissal.

Annunciation Junior High had been plagued by rival teens from a nearby school. We never knew when to send a faculty member to "street duty," acting as a deterrent to a potential street fight. Rumor was today was one of those days.

Earlier we enjoyed a lively discussion of how the Silva techniques could affect the aggressive behavior within ourselves and that of our neighboring students. The students' reflections were brilliant:

- *"We got more confidence."*
- *"They be talkin' lies about us."*
- *"We got that confident smile and we be thinkin' 'cancel-cancel.'"*
- *"We got the three-finger technique."*
- *"We be centered and all cool lookin'."*

I laughed, enjoying the naiveite of teens coupled with their deep wisdom.

The three o-clock dismissal bell rang harshly. This was the day the kids would mentally take on the nearby rivals. This day they would truly test the power of their minds to control their environment. This day they would experience that self-control, not retaliatory violence, works best.

They quickly demonstrated there is a power in the universe greater than we are and we can use it. The drama was over quickly, as a handful of our boys stood right in the middle of the street, took the taunts, smiled, and refrained from physically engaging. A peak day for me as an educator, I could not have been prouder.

A full fifty years later, while sitting in a Denver diner, an older, Latina waitress, cocked her head and said inquisitively, "Sister Kathleen, is that you?" Although fifty years influences an 8th grader's looks, I did recognize her name and that of the family, instantly.

Her dominant story was remembering when the boys used Silva techniques to survive, yes thrive, in the street. "That day, we got that meditation stuff and using your head really does work." My heart soared yet again.

These experiences trigger me to ask what stories in my life would be served by eliminating them as no longer true. What stories can I reframe to be the supportive story worth telling?

They say we die twice, once when our bodily functions stop, and again when they stop telling our stories. What transformative value is available when we control how our stories are told?

WILLINGNESS TO LET GO

When stories are told about us, we tend to believe them. Who knows us better than family? There is no human being on the planet who knows me better than my brother. He literally has known me since my birth. His stories about me matter. They must be true. Even though I believe his interpretation, my job is to be discreet and willing to let go.

So is yours. Maturity led you to the position of choice. Your legacy is composed of your stories, and you can create it as desired. Thus, I invite you to release any story that does not serve you or that brings harm to any sentient being. The following is a real-life story to put the power of that release into perspective.

HATING MATH

As a student I found school difficult, especially math. With my best math grade a C, I admit to the presence of Ds and Fs over the years. The kind and gentle Sisters of Charity designed a high school track using general

*math. College prep courses in algebra, geome-
try, or calculus were deemed too difficult. I felt
grateful at the time, as it was the appropriate
course.*

*Once I graduated and entered the Sisters of
Charity, it was time to release the low self-esteem. The expectation of college attendance and
success dominated. The community provided
necessary assistance for all the young sisters'
successes.*

I carefully made it through college, began
teaching (including math), and ultimately started
my own financial planning firm. Pretty good for
the kid struggling with poor math self-esteem.
Pretty good for the woman willing to transform
her old stories. Pretty good for the power of
having people believe in you.

As a budding entrepreneur, what might be
a deterrent in your path? I know no one who is
strong in all the competing skill sets. You may
flourish with effective people skills yet lack
mechanical prowess. You may be a crackerjack
with remembering details but hate being around
people socially.

An indication of preference is to look at how

you refresh. Imagine the end of a long and challenging day. Is your dominant choice to go out drinking with friends, or do you yearn to go home, be quiet, and recoup? Knowing how you are is invaluable. Having someone believe in you just as you are is invaluable. Hiring someone with the expertise you lack is invaluable.

BEAT YOUR HEAD AGAINST A BRICK WALL

An excellent example of growing into the strengths you own while acknowledging your less preferred strengths is captured in this following story.

Russell, my father, had a heritage that would be described as German, Catholic, lower-class, frustrated entrepreneur who never made it to high school. Yet he was brilliant in his natural mathematical and critical-thinking capabilities. Owning a demolition and salvage business, Dad could look at a building, figure in his head the amount of time, employee costs, trips to the city dump, fees, and taxes. He then calculated anticipated funds from selling the used building materials. Now he was ready to bid the costs for demolition. Rarely did he lose a bid to a competitor and his work was lauded as fair, complete, and on time.

Russell not being home for dinner meant one thing. After a tiring day of demolition, he often stopped at a favored tavern for Jack Daniels or several Rolling Rock beers. At home the tension became palpable as we gobbled down dinner hoping to be finished before he appeared.

With my two brothers in the room, we collectively knew what infractions we had committed that day. Dad would viciously yell, "You kids are so stupid. Beat your stupid heads against a brick wall." I could see the sweet release in his face. Add an evening six pack and any stories of explanation, defiance, or resistance triggered the belt coming off.

My math skills were never comparable to his natural ability, so it was easy to own his harsh assessment of my intelligence. Is my history of acquiring two master's degrees, a doctorate, and multiple lines of professional certifications truly the love of learning or just showing Russell he was wrong about me? Perhaps it is both.

As you transition to new career opportunities, you get to choose if your old beliefs support your efforts. You get to let go of any story that does not support you. You do so by canceling, forgiving, releasing, and reframing those incorrect interpretations of your life. Spoiler alert! You get to manage your own internal weather.

YOUR PAST SUCCESS
Being Your Best

I love feeling sassy and when I do, I wear a hat. It's like saying, "Hey, look at me. I'm both sassy and a force to be reckoned with." It feels great to be confident and successful. Whether as a boss, parent, or friend, you love being the best you can be. As you proceed into your new venture, expect nothing less of yourself. The sweetness of knowing you can deliver is one of life's treats, as I recently experienced.

The air felt damp and bone chillingly cold, typical for a Cincinnati winter morning. A few college buddies got together for our annual holiday breakfast to catch up and reminisce. There are always gems available in these precious encounters, especially as we become aware when one of us transitions. When will it be my turn, I wondered?

The pensive look on my friend's face revealed her thoughtful musing, "Kathleen, you always inspire me. Over the years I've noticed you've changed careers, from teaching to marketing, marketing to finance, finance to ministry. You've honored your dreams, took on unbelievable challenges, and created success in all that. Now we're all in our seventies and most of us are retired. We can look back at our successes and realize we created lives worth living. I love that you just keep creating the next phase. Now an ordained minister, you go off and get your doctorate of divinity. You're like the energizer bunny. You just don't stop."

Having someone outside yourself mirroring back life's patterns is powerful. You tend to believe the perception coming from another. As a budding entrepreneur, you must be solidly grounded in what those strengths are. You will pull from and rely on them in your future travels. It matters not what others think. You are grounded in who you really are.

The Gifts You Bring

Transformational guru Rev. Cynthia James had her students record on an index card five God qualities that people revealed as theirs. Taking on the perception others hold of me, I proudly wrote: happy, prosperous, energetic, confident, and healthy.

Then we were instructed to write, "And this is the beginning of my day." That was powerful. Taped to my mirror, it is a daily reminder about how life is for me.

Care to try this experiment? Reflect on descriptors of you at your best. Reflect on qualities you know are true of the Divine. Reflect on the positive aspects of you shared from family and friends. Therein lies a rich and personalized list. Review the list, choosing the five dominant aspects of you. Be careful not to choose those aspects you wish were yours. Choose who you are in this moment.

Display your list with the reminder, "This is the beginning of my day." You can use it as a screensaver, post it on your mirror, place it in your billfold, or put it anywhere you will see it regularly. Be as public or as private as you wish.

Taking personality assessments is an effective

way to learn about yourself, especially your mental, behavioral, spiritual, and emotional self. From these, much self-confidence is available. The Emergenetics assessment tool is a favorite, as it looks at internal and external factors. Myers-Briggs, DISC Behavior Inventory, Gallup's Clifton Strength's Assessment, and Situational Judgment Tests are all on an extensive list available for professionals, employers, and individuals.

Over the years, I have taken numerous personality evaluations. I encourage you to engage in similar objective feedback to help identify your unique qualities and characteristics. It helps you anticipate the challenges of being an entrepreneur and strengthens your useable traits in professional and personal areas of your life.

To access several, ask friends and colleagues which of their own traits have made a significant difference for them. Google "personal assessment tools" and you find a plethora. It is well worth your time. Remember Socrates: "The unexamined life is not worth living."

On Happiness

We live in a culture willing to show our shadow side. That side is exploited through weekly television dramas and the daily news. We are bombarded with negativity. Recently I became aware of how much I enjoy the intrigue of cop stories, who-done-it mysteries, the drama of murders, rapes, and exciting techniques of police work. Simultaneously, I realized the volume of these socially unacceptable behaviors I indulge in while watching television. How is this affecting my consciousness, my expectation of other's behavior, my own sense of morality?

This became clear to me at 4:30 AM, when I awakened with the feelings of rage, frustration, and struggle. I knew horrific events are not OK in my value system. I felt helpless and victimized. Examples swirling in my mind seemed real – if scenes from TV scriptwriters, producers, and actors can be real.

Yuck. I had just indulged in binge-watching a favorite crime series with strong graphics. Numerous acts of inhumanity polluted the gruesome scripts. My mind is affected whether real or labeled "entertainment." I realized how many murders and rapes I view in the name of entertainment.

Something needed to be done. I made a commitment to watch less violence in entertainment and engage a discipline within myself to see the good and praise it.

NEW ADVENTURES TO BEGIN

Each morning shepherds in a day of incredible opportunities, adventures, and excitement. Why? Because you say so. That passion for this new career is giving your voice the lilt, joy, and volume to be heard majestically. What will your voice say to your world?

Power Starting Your Day

I spent 13 years as a Catholic Sister of Charity, receiving innumerable gifts that totally shifted the focus of my life. One that continues to serve me is the non-negotiable habit of a sacred morning routine. This is where self-care starts for me: sipping a cup of hot coffee, meditating, journaling, praying, reading spiritual or personal growth pieces.

This is a precious beginning for each day. His Holiness the Dalai Lama, when presented with a stressful schedule, noted the need to pray twice as long that morning.

Do you start your day in ways both pleasing and powerful? Is your morning ritual tinged with pleasure, fun, energy? If it is ideal, yay! If not, what would you like it to be?

Law of Attraction

Highly successful entrepreneurs describe how they start each day. They declare to the universe that their day is awesome, their activities joyous, their successes outrageously prosperous. Delivered silently or aloud, the effect of setting the day's energetic field is palpable.

Write your own creative message that will thrill you each time you deliver it. Play with this until you nail it powerfully.

As you continue through the day, be critically aware of the power of your thoughts. What you allow yourself to think, you tend to attract. With that understanding, choose to attract friendship, prosperity, and kindness.

It is said that you can tell the dominant pattern of your past thoughts by looking at your life's experiences and current level of prosperity. These are great indicators of your dominant thought patterns. My bumper sticker reads, "Thoughts Become Things. Choose the Good Ones." Be sensitive to what you allow yourself to think. It dramatically affects the success of your business, the loyalty of employees, and the enthusiasm of investors.

Energy from Passion

Over the years, I realized that exhaustion from my day was often linked to the degree of negativity, challenge, and upset I experienced. I also realized that on the days I controlled my reactions, the result was an energy I cherished. I did this by deliberately thinking of the good and praising it.

Being able to control your energy level for your new passion is an entrepreneur's greatest task. You no longer have a boss, coworkers' expectations, or corporate scheduling demands to act as outside motivators.

You are up to creating your own energy from the passion of your vision. You are up to creating your own sustainability by the smart moves you incorporate as healthy daily habits. You are up to experiencing a depth of joy by understanding your strengths and using them.

POINTS TO PONDER/QUESTIONS TO JOURNAL

1. What would I get from the exercise of writing my childhood memories? Should

I share them with a trusted soul? Is my control strengthened by choosing to dissolve, reframe, or celebrate those stories?

2. I want a personality assessment so I will find the one that fits me best, take it, and share the results—or not.

3. I can assess my greatest strengths, evaluate how they affect my entrepreneurial activity, and be willing to attract those with skill sets I lack. I get that my job should be fun.

4. I will determine my God-qualities from my own private meditation or through asking trusted people. I will allow awareness of my strengths to energize me throughout my day.

5. Would starting my day with a fun, energetic, and positive ritual really shift my life? I will experiment with this to see.

CHAPTER TWO

Know Your Numbers

ESSENTIAL TO OUTRAGEOUS success for any entrepreneur is to know your numbers. Here is your real-world guide to the reality of marketing, the framework of success, and the effectiveness of your passion. You can objectively look at your business, know it is so much more than a hobby, and relish your expertise. A common saying is *"successful people are willing to be measured."* That is you!

FUNDAMENTALS OF FINANCIAL SUCCESS

Like most newly minted entrepreneurs, you can easily get caught up in the newness, expanded learning, and ego satisfaction of finally doing what your heart desires. All those dynamics are simultaneously tamed and encouraged when you are in command of the numbers.

True entrepreneurs love knowing where they are. They love the confidence they have as they take their projections to the local banker for loan assessments. They relish their self-confidence as the numbers expand with business growth. They appreciate knowing where they came from as they celebrate even minor improvements.

Eliminating Naiveté

Not knowing your numbers leaves you vulnerable. Without a firm grasp of your numbers, you might make knee-jerk decisions that could be financially detrimental. Without understanding where you are and where you are headed, unsupportive decisions could easily be made. They can be deceptive, given your excitement over the new direction in your life. You are excited to share your new venture with family and friends, and often elicit their feedback. Being the master of your numbers is a powerful way to stave off the naiveté inherent in new directions and the opinions of others.

When I was leaving the Sisters of Charity, a lay colleague at school started a new part-time position working for a financial company. As practice, she offered to consult with me. I felt so grateful. Within minutes, she had suggestions. "Create a savings account. That old $500 car you just financed will need repairs, new tires, etc. Have the money in savings so you don't need to borrow." "Brilliant," I thought, "of course."

Her second and major advice was to immediately buy a million-dollar whole-life insurance policy. Financial naiveté was my reality but intuitively I knew a single, healthy, thirty-ish woman with no one financially dependent on her should not justify significant premiums for that kind of death benefit. I needed money to get gas in my old clunker.

She did not make an insurance sale, yet I did start a savings account.

Financial Maturity

Being a wise steward of money is the core of financial maturity. It begins with setting aside the fear of knowing. Seriously, *set aside the fear of knowing*. Some people experience financial knowledge as inhibiting their ecstatic sense of freedom.

Here is an example. Someone says to you, "You've got a great idea there. Just go for it and worry about paying for it later. You're not getting any younger, so make hay while the sun shines." The element of immaturity in that perspective can be devastating. Your challenge is to enthusiastically act on great ideas supported by a solid financial plan.

Most entrepreneurs are risk takers. They frequently live on the cutting edge and can tolerate doing so. For those later-in-life entrepreneurs who are used to decades of stability, guaranteed paychecks, faux comfort in a structure of corporate buck-passing, and a culture of organization and profitability, life on the edge is not necessarily comfortable.

All entrepreneurs are not *ipso facto* risk takers. To understand and totally accept where you are regarding risk is a precious gift you give yourself.

Newer entrepreneurs find it unsettling to finance a fledging business venture using credit cards with interest rates ranging from eight to twenty-four percent. It is fiscally disastrous to use qualified retirement savings accounts (a 401(k), 403(b), or an IRA), losing potentially forty percent of each dollar to early withdrawal penalties and federal and state taxes. It is unsettling to ravage the kids' college education account. Financing for the newly minted entrepreneur calls for different strategies.

This is where working with a financial advisor or a small business coach is extremely valuable. Look for sources of available income from present cash flow, opportunities to reduce periodic over-payments to the IRS, evaluating what is important in family expenditures and what can be modified. These are all great places to start.

For many businesses, financing options through banks and the Small Business Administration offer advantages. Wealthy parents willing to make an early gift of inheritance money could be an option. Talk with your financial advisor and your banker to brainstorm options.

You may be surprised how influential and generous friends can be. Consider the learning experiences inherent in my entering the business world from the comfortable confines of community living.

What did I know about waitressing in a tavern? What I did know is I could not financially survive on a Catholic school teacher's salary of $2,000 a year. After I left the convent, parents of students came out of the woodwork to lend a hand. One offered a cashier's job at Wilson's House of Leather and Suede, another a waitress position at Sutera's Restaurant in Aurora, Colorado. I took them both.

I continued to teach junior high school in Denver. Being in my late thirties made working three jobs more challenging than if I were twenty-two. My rewards were significant. I carried no credit card debt, had sufficient income to cover meager expenses, and learned the strength to survive on my own. YES!

Then that was challenged. "Someone just came in, you're next," bellowed restaurateur John Sutera. Approaching the table, I stopped breathing as I felt weak kneed and completely out of control. Does a male human specimen get any better looking than this? Tall, thin, elegant, regal, confident, with that chiseled chin, sexy white hair, and a charming Boston accent to boot. Hello!

While presenting his drink, I asked," So what are you reading?" "You wouldn't get it," he teasingly replied. "It's a man's book." I felt challenged. That challenging reaction diminished when he inquired whether I was working the next night.

As a sophisticated businessman, Bob Mulhern became my anchor through the evolution from nonprofit service-based employment to experiencing the business world. The practical focus on dress for success, business card usage, explaining what I did using a call to action—all were gifts my new mentor lavished on me. Deeply grateful, I followed his coaching closely, wanting him to be so proud of me. Then he was not.

My faux pas embarrassed Bob and my unconsciousness could not figure out why. I landed a sales position with ABDick selling printing presses, very much a man's world. Two full intense weeks of training in Chicago ensued. I was the only woman in a class of thirty men. This is how it unfolded.

- Who is your typical client? Local entrepreneurs who own their own corner printing company experienced only with male salespeople.
- What is your target product? The ABDick 360 offset printing press.
- Learn the features, advantages, and benefits of the mainstay product. Know your competition and their products.

Post this, I was assured my success would be enhanced because I was a woman.

Enthused with new possibilities and a headful of facts, I failed to recognize the degree of the male culture I had assumed. Unknowingly affected by that learning environment, I unconsciously assumed the language of young men in the printing industry.

Returning home from Chicago, I was anxious to have dinner with Bob. Unfortunately, his twenty-three-year-old daughter was in town and excited to meet me. Dinner was a disaster. I sensed she grew uncomfortable throughout our time together and realized I would never have her vote to be "Dad's best friend."

I felt exposed and embarrassed when later Bob coached me on the number of times I used the word f*ck, with enthusiasm, during our dinner conversation. What? His daughter was blown away, he was mortified, and I remained unconscious of such a vagrant faux pas. Lesson learned.

CHART YOUR COURSE
Make It Fun

For many, financial challenges can be overwhelming and discouraging. Here is where self-care, humor, balance, and patience are used to continue life's fun. Keep yourself surrounded with people who are patient and humorous. A professional money coach can keep it light while directing your valuable time and energy. Connecting with local entrepreneur support groups is also helpful.

Above all, have fun, stay light, and remain energized. Keep in mind the WHY of your vision. Why are you taking your life in this direction?

Keeping it fun includes riding the wave of change with ease and grace. Being an entrepreneur will automatically open the door for change to be rampant in your life.

Take, for example, my history. Immediately after leaving teaching as a Sister of Charity, I landed a job selling offset printing presses through ABDick Co. There was a small printing company on every corner, all in need of equipment and daily supplies. Today, it can be difficult to even find an offset printer. Yet computer-driven copy services abound. Things change.

When large grocery chains and big box stores emerged, we mourned the loss of the corner grocery store. Yet, today there seems to be a 7-11 on every corner. Things change.

When I was a young financial advisor, the investment milieu dictated minimal cash reserves and strong positions in high-yield junk bonds. Things change.

Why are you drawn to be an entrepreneur in the industry you are attracted to? How is it in alignment with your core values, your desire for prosperity, and your ability to make a difference? Does it support your desire to have fun?

Desire for Accountability

Getting a great accountant, bookkeeper, or financial advisor is a smart move. Loving, supportive professionals give us a framework in which to flourish. We can share our frustrations, delight in our successes, and muse about our place in the world, and they understand.

Personal accountability also is powerful. When I know I will be accountable at the next meeting, I am more motivated to act. When I allow another to give me ideas, my vision of the goal and the process of getting there expands.

Accountability is important and can be supported even with a commitment to periodic journaling.

Accountability to a partner or spouse is

powerful. I recommend a Friday date night where spouses take time monthly to review their goals, discuss issues they struggle with, pay bills together, make cash flow decisions, and celebrate the growth in their accounts.

I recommend periodic meetings among business partners to provide the growth, progress, success stories, finances, and exciting new ideas for the business. Wherever you have people who support you, therein lie opportunities for accountability, education, and celebration.

Attract the Perfect Professional

We most often hire a professional based on a recommendation from a colleague, friend, or family member. If you need a tax professional, look for a Certified Public Accountant (CPA) or an Enrolled Agent. Both can stand in for you during an audit and have specific IRS training to do so.

If you want a financial advisor/coach, check out your state's Financial Planning Association website. This unique organization is composed of Certified Financial Planners (CFPs) committed to staying professionally sharp by interfacing with colleagues for strong networking.

You want to pay for counseling, not be limited

to investment recommendations without business development advice. There is no reason to play small when it comes to your business and your life. You are the beloved child of the Most High and it is in your best interest to *be* the best while being surrounded *by* the best. Remember who you are.

Riding That Emotional Rollercoaster

Let's presume that all professionals come with excellent credentials. What you are looking for is the person who will ride your emotional rollercoaster while kicking your butt and holding your hand. To find this emotionally and spiritually compatible person, I recommend you interview at least three candidates. If they are all equally credentialed, then you are free to evaluate with your intuitive sense to find that compatibility factor.

Give yourself the freedom to explore. You are not marrying them. If a different fit comes up later, go for it. This work you do is important. Get coaching from the best.

IT'S LONELY AT THE TOP

Ultimately, each decision is yours. The work is yours. The successes are yours. The legacy is yours. Allow it to reflect the awesomeness you bring to the world.

While you work smartly, experience successes, and create your legacy, be sure you enjoy the journey, not just the destination. Pay attention to self-care. Keep yourself surrounded with family who loves you, and friends who are fun and loyal. This keeps the noted challenges of being an entrepreneur in balance.

Take an Objective Look

What is your conflict management style? Often evaluations can be birthed from outside ourselves. These are frequently imposed through an authority figure who feels some right to determine what your value is. Wrong!

Consider the story of my godfather.

Grandma's apartment house, affectionately known as "43" for 436 W. Jefferson Street, was the scene of a scary encounter. I snuggled on the living room couch, since this was my bedroom at age five. My drunken father, Russell, reigned at the living room table perched next to the windows. Across the table and equally soused, was his best friend, my godfather, Joe.

Dad wanted to be right about judging Joe as a loser, because he was a government employee and Dad a true, courageous entrepreneur. Joe wanted some respect from his friend and to end the nightmare of humiliation Russell so perceptively dished out.

Both men raised their voices louder and louder. There was no television in the apartment to drown out their vulgar arguing. Mother tried feverishly to interrupt their escalating angry exchange to no avail. I just wanted to not be there. How could I disappear?

The pot of pent-up emotions and old wounds began boiling faster. I felt afraid. Am I safe being here on my bed, the open couch in the living room? I felt vulnerable.

As the anger peaked, my father took his mustard drenched hot dog and threw it at Joe. Not a pretty sight with yellow goop smeared all over Joe's shirt and disgrace smearing his soul. Did ridiculing my godfather help Dad feel better?

I learned I do not like the tension of friends fighting. I also learned incorrectly that working for the federal government meant you were a lazy son-of-a-gun and not worth much. I bought into the idea that being an entrepreneur, like my Dad, was so far superior. Not true.

We all get to assess and reframe our beliefs from childhood. We ask if any belief serves our highest and best interest. If I find that it does, I celebrate it, value it, and am desirous to share it as part of my legacy. Notice what you say to your kids, as though it is gospel. Is that the legacy you are proud of?

If a belief is no longer in concert with your current value system, you get to choose. You can reframe it to be in harmony with what's true for you now, or drop it entirely, or make up a new one. Life is not about what happens to you but what you say about what happened. You co-create your life with every passing thought. You get to choose.

Determine your own success based on what is in your highest and best interests. Only you know what will make your heart sing. Only you can adequately judge the inherent value of your services. An objective yet supportive evaluation is all that is required.

Being Judged by Your Numbers

Selectivity regarding who gets access to your business plan and corresponding financials is paramount to your success. You want the real numbers and appropriate strategies, while avoiding any negativity. If someone discourages you financially, run! But run to a professional who can show you the how and the timetable—and can do so with enthusiasm. You may be your own worst enemy when it comes to critical behaviors, so show yourself compassion, understanding, and gentleness.

Knowing your numbers is not inherently problematic. There may be great joy in knowing your accurate numbers. Take, for example, a beloved client couple. Both enjoyed the teacher's pension system and experienced the ever-popular belief that educators are paid poorly. They were incredibly discouraged. I chose to raise their consciousness regarding the power of their retirement package and calculated their retirement numbers.

This was challenging given what I was hearing from them: "We'll never make it on just our pension after all these years of working. It's not fair. We could have saved in our 403(b), which we did some but not enough. Now we're just plain tired and want to hang it up. We feel trapped. By the time we retire we'll be too old to enjoy it. Wouldn't it be awesome to travel abroad other than just in the summer months?"

The iconic "Four Percent Rule" was an eye opener for them. How big of a portfolio would you need for it to last your lifetime? They had no idea. I explained, "If you want $40,000 annual income you need a low-risk account of one million dollars. At four percent, one million dollars would yield you forty thousand. Since there are two of you, and your current spending is $120,000 annually, you're looking at a three-million-dollar portfolio, in which you take the risk and never get a raise. If you factor in cost of living increases, a desired guaranteed income, and no personal market risks, how big of a portfolio would you need?" It was all so confusing.

I invited them to come back in a week so I could get to work crunching their numbers. Their precious pension yielded eighty-two percent of current salary, came with peace of mind knowing it was a tax-backed pension, included raises for cost of living, and absorbed the investment risks so they did not. Whew! Allowing for the 403(b) balance, I factored in higher medical costs and a healthy travel budget, allowing for trips in the fall and spring. I was excited the day they returned.

On a crisp October morning, I suggested they submit their retirement papers effective for the end of that school year. The numbers showed this could easily be their last academic year working. In disbelief, they sat staring at me. They said they needed to think about this, and then they did it. The following September I received a postcard from Florence, Italy. It was inscribed with a thank you for helping them see their vision while they were still young enough to travel whenever they wished.

Get your numbers crunched so you are grounded in the truth of where you are and what it takes to realize your vision. You deserve nothing less.

Know What Makes You Happy

A business plan has many moving parts. As an entrepreneur you get to design it in concert with your joy. You make it personal when you consistently ask, "Will this bring me joy?" Apply that criteria to money spent, the time you are willing to give, which markets you are comfortable approaching, and services you choose to render.

Knowing this will allow you to design a life you love living. Ask often, "Will this bring me joy?"

Celebrate Your Successes

Plan your success markers. This breaks down the daunting bigger goals into attainable realistic ones. Once achieved, what is an authentic celebration? Make it viable. Having a manicure as a reward marker for me is useless. My standard appointment at the nail salon is already in place. However, a day at my favorite spa would be a treat, while a drive in the mountains is heavenly.

Know yourself. Make it real. If not truly motivational, it is useless.

POINTS TO PONDER/QUESTIONS TO JOURNAL

1. It takes courage to know your numbers. We are afraid they will not be good enough and we will be overwhelmed with what it would take to be successful. Set aside that FEAR (**F**alse **E**vidence **A**ppearing **R**eal) and get a professional to run your numbers.

2. Balance realistic risk with financial naiveté. Know your risk tolerance and how to plan the financing of your vision. Stay open to surprises from the universe.

3. Networking is your powerful tool. Who will you share your vision with? Whose advice do you trust and cherish? Who will you seek out?

4. Who can be your accountability coach(es)? Ask them in such a way that they are honored to be part of your journey.

5. Your job is to have fun twice, once while you are working and again in your success celebrations. What brings you joy?

CHAPTER THREE

Who Are You Helping?

YOUR IDEAL CLIENT

Clarity around what you desire is one of the powerful aids in our own achievement. Being crystal clear about who you serve eliminates the wanderings of your mind, energy, and precious revenue.

Being in vibrational alignment with your desired good allows the universe to take your request seriously. It also allows you to be articulate with your elevator speech, describing your business in the time it takes for an elevator ride. Hearing your explanation of what you do, how you serve, and who your ideal client is a show-stopper every time you deliver it.

Stop Saving the World: Be Selective

No, you do not want the whole world as potential clients. It is not your challenge to save or serve everyone. It is your privilege to attract those who are ready for you and your services.

This is the classic discussion of niche marketing. Be willing to change your understanding of your niche market so it evolves as you evolve.

Do your research. Who are your competitors and what clientele do they serve? What demographics describe their clientele in terms of age, gender, educational background, economic status? Determine whether your services will target the same groups or if there is a niche just waiting to be filled.

At any given time, have clarity around what that market is for you in the present moment. Through your clarity you are helping make a world that works for everyone.

Being in Vibrational Alignment

Being in vibrational alignment with your goal through intellectual clarity and realistic emotions makes you unstoppable. As an entrepreneur, I attest to the power of being eager for the universe to flood us with goodness. Sounds great—and how do we do that?

Most of the time we are overwhelmed with the tasks of maintaining a clear vision, being fiscally responsible, exercising powerful yet compassionate leadership skills, and working twelve hours a day. I asked my online Prosperity Plus class to describe "vibrational alignment." Here are a few of their stellar responses:

Karen: It's a feeling. Imagine it. See yourself IN it through contemplation and visualization. Enjoy the vision with great gratitude.

Carolyn: What you are grateful for is already done. Take inspired action and feel the visceral tingling.

Pam: The gifts have already been given. Let them in. Be specific and clear, then declare "this or something better." Leave the HOW to the universe.

Mallika: My thoughts, words, and actions

need to speak my vision.

Geoffrey: Knowing my whole life is of God, I experience magnificence.

What is your definition?

Vibrational alignment is being in concert with your goal through intellectual clarity and realistic emotions. Once you have an experiential consciousness of how this works, be willing to dive deep. Apply this skill to your clients.

This is magical. Imagine the very people you intend to serve being in vibrational alignment with their best interests. Given the nature of your services, how could you facilitate that awareness in them?

Start with how you facilitated that awareness in yourself. Experiment with your answer. Can you imagine a more authentic, powerful, and relevant conversation to have with clients? Can you imagine the relevance you and your services will have in their lives?

This, or Something Better

Stay open to surprises. Entrepreneurs with fantastic imaginations can be lulled into thinking their ideas are challenging for the universe. I love the saying: "Want to make God laugh? Share your plans with Him." Opposite that, or for those with little imagination, the quiet fear of manifesting mediocracy is prevalent. What if both imagination and mediocracy are irrelevant?

A more powerful path would be to do your visioning, which includes your vibrational alignment work, developing your smart business plan, and then declaring confidently, "This, or something better."

EFFECTIVE NETWORKING

The universe provides for your needs in a myriad of ways. One of the most notable is the direct meeting of colleagues, friends, and, yes, strangers. "Surprise! Aha! Can you actually believe I just met them?"

In these happenstance encounters, you meet the perfect people to aid your success. How does this happen with such ease and grace? Having the intention and simply showing up are keys.

Happenstance, Accidents, and Serendipity

Networking is one of the universe's way of communicating. Isn't it powerful to run into someone who is the perfect recipient of your services, who deeply appreciates you, and who is easily capable of paying for your expertise, guidance, and experience? How does that happen? What are the effective modalities for people to learn about your work, availability, and remuneration?

The universe conspires for our success. Being aware and then grateful are two active agents to employ in our relationship with the Divine. As you expand in vibrational alignment, you tend to become a magnet for even more of these so-called happenstances or accidents.

Developing your intuitive skill set is a huge asset. Add present-moment mindfulness and deep gratitude to expand your capacity to receive both gifts more fully.

Your greatest challenges can also be your greatest teachers. It takes courage to unlearn what you have known to be true, even sacred. You need to make room for a new way of thinking, a new vision of yourself.

Going from a junior-high teacher in an urban Catholic school to a printing press salesperson, in a man's competitive world, caused me to have a dramatic shift in my self-image. For thirteen years, I was accustomed to a feminine world where I was revered, respected, and honored. Suddenly I was hustling in a male-dominated competitive world of grease and printing ink. It was glorious!

Hold on. The universe was not done with me.

Through a quirk of happenstance my broker friend, Jane, introduced me to a gentleman destined to change the trajectory of my life. We often would set up lunch or a drink after work to introduce each other to a man we thought may be interesting.

Such was the purpose of lunch one day at the Brown Palace. I was impressed with the iconic, high-end venue, given it was a perfect celebration for a gigantic accomplishment of the morning. One of my largest accounts, Coors Brewery, had just a signed purchase order for ABDick's latest and largest printing equipment that included a computer to run the production. Unbelievable! A computer within a printing press! Talk about cutting edge. It was the first sold from our branch, and after lunch I would be delivering the order to my sales manager.

I was electrified as I met Phil Mortimer. My sneaky broker friend, Jane, had set up Mr.

Mortimer to interview me for a sales position in his company. Thinking this was a social time, I thought it strange he asked questions like, "Where do you see yourself in five years, and how do you feel when you close a sale?" He thoroughly quizzed me on the electric feeling of having that equipment order in my purse.

Before lunch was completed, Mr. Mortimer had closed on me. I was to be his guest in Reno, Nevada, shadowing one of his salesmen specializing in financial services for educators. It took only one day to realize that being in service to fellow teachers, using math skills daily, and making a huge difference in clients' lives is exactly what my heart yearned for.

Law of Attraction

The powerful law attracting desired connections, breaks, and opportunities is commonly referred to as the Law of Attraction. It is enhanced through clarity of what you truly want and being in vibrational alignment with your good. This crystal-clear goal comes alive with emotional support gleaned from the deliberate use of all five senses. You may want a Porsche convertible, so see yourself in the driver's seat, feeling comfortable, looking hot, being confident and excited. Make it come alive.

Clarity around what is physically desired allows the Law of Attraction to find a welcome home. To put the law on steroids, go beyond the physical manifestation. Have clarity around your resulting feelings with the ultimate result of acquisition. What goes on in vagueness stays in vagueness.

Include feelings on your list of desires. Do not limit it to physical traits.

If you want a well-described life partner, your intended results might be security, companionship, love, financial peace of mind, etc. Thus, when you create a vision board, the resulting feelings of each manifestation could hold a dominant space on that board. Imagine that: a vision board of desired feelings!

To tell the truth, it was the promise of tea and free cookies at the May Company that lured my friend Nancy and me to hear a woman talk about money. A woman! Talking about money? Highly unusual in the 1970s. It was all Greek to me.

Yet, I left with three important insights:

First was the overriding realization that there was a volume of information unavailable to me. I have an inquiring mind. I wanted to know.

Second was the inspiration from two professional, articulate women in their grey suits and business pumps. They impressed me.

Third was a deep sense of gratitude for their generosity setting up this educational experience, providing tea and cookies, and offering to meet personally. "I'm so grateful you chose to join me today. I would be privileged to extend our educational experience by meeting with you personally."

Being two new and struggling salespeople from ABDick Co, we were pleased the appointment was complementary. It took little prep for this personal meeting. Jane, the broker, became more baffled, finally asking, "I don't understand. You're a professional woman, in your later thirties, with only a checking account. There's no savings, property, retirement funds, or investments. And the only insurance is on the old car you needed to finance. This indicates interesting experiences with finances. Tell me more."

"It's called a vow of poverty," I sheepishly revealed.

She interrupted my sharing with, "Oh, my God, I'm talking to an ex-nun. Let's wind this up and go for a drink." The Cricket Tavern in Denver's Cherry Creek district became the birthplace for a great, influential, and enduring friendship.

ARTICULATE YOUR GIFTS

Once the universe generously provides connections, you want to step into that arena with ease and grace. This is where your elevator speech enables you to articulate who you are and the huge difference you make in our world. Done smartly and with enthusiasm, you become a magnet for greater good, and your self-confidence is enhanced.

There are many tried-and-true modalities for writing an elevator speech. Use whichever one speaks to you. Consider adding an initial step. In an elevator speech, you present the best of you to your world. Being crystal clear in knowing what your personal dynamics are and feeling charged up knowing them will leave you masterful at both the content and the delivery.

Begin with a meditative experience and list twenty or more of what you consider to be your God qualities. It is said you cannot recognize said qualities unless they already exist within you.

Choose five from your list and prayerfully be with them. Which do you know are true and which have come to you from others? Both are valuable. Now examine which three could be woven into your elevator speech. Design your talk around those God qualities you wish to communicate to your world.

Regardless of which modality works best for you, remember that your pitch should be as short as what you could deliver during an elevator ride.

Let the World Know

Perhaps using a business coach to help you construct and deliver your key business components is a gift worth giving yourself.

Once completed, consider social media as an excellent delivery system for a succinct explanation of who you are, how you benefit those you serve, and how you expect to be compensated.

Enthusiastic networking with target groups allows people to interface with the real you. As you connect with entrepreneurs in your profession, you will be enriched with a myriad of ideas. Listen, evaluate them, and incorporate those that fit.

Shout It from the Rooftops

Once written, your declaration of who you are and how you are making a huge difference can be shouted throughout the social media world. It can be on your website, at the end of every blog post, and included as a footnote to every correspondence. A tight and powerful articulation of you is worth its weight in gold.

Determine how people in your industry have found success. Expand that by thinking in ways unique to you.

Shout It to Your Soul

You are your most important client and best friend. You ultimately are the source of your own motivation, energy field, enthusiasm, creativity, and discipline. As an independent entrepreneur, you do not have the corporate structure to frame where you will work and what hours you will be present. There is no hierarchy of command. When something goes wrong, *you* are the chain of command. The buck stops with you.

There are no departments that specialize in hiring. You learn the regulations, deal with all governmental agencies, conduct the interviews, and pay the person. There is no payroll department issuing you a guaranteed salary.

There is a marketing department – you. If strategizing, design, and technology are not your skillsets, marketing still must be done.

As you progress with your vision, you will need friends, family, and support staff to align with your vision, bringing their expertise to bear on your behalf.

Make sure you spend your time using your strengths and enjoying the journey.

There is an iconic story of the village woman known far and wide for her exceptionally delicious pies. She loved baking, experimenting, and offering a grateful village her culinary creations. As her fame grew, the suggestion came to expand, making her coveted pies more widely available. Pleased with the villager's appreciation, she did exactly that. In a short period, she found herself deluged with ordering supplies, training chefs, coordinating distribution systems, leaving her stuck in a small office running her new company. She desperately missed baking pies. She was miserable.

You have a burning passion that motivates

you to leave a more structured environment and engage in baking your own pies. You may be the stellar masseuse, coach, or psychic. Give thought to surrounding yourself with a cadre of people who share your vision. Allow yourself to continue doing what you love, what you are good at, and what makes you happy.

Be responsible for your own joy. Shout it to your own soul.

POINTS TO PONDER/QUESTIONS TO JOURNAL

1. Write an in-depth description of your ideal client. Have the intention that this is the focus of your attention.

2. To be a vibrational match for your good requires intellectual clarity and matching emotions. Be in vibrational alignment with your entrepreneurial success. Write it. Speak to it. Be it.

3. Put the Law of Attraction on steroids. Attach feeling outcomes to your desires. Journal this, share it, live it.

4. Create your elevator speech based on your dominant strengths.

5. Shout your value, services, and intentions first and often to yourself. Smart marketing will naturally follow.

CHAPTER FOUR

Making Money

*Life is a mirror and will reflect back
to the thinker what he thinks into it.*
—Ernest Holmes

CONDUCT YOUR RESEARCH

Until clients experience your uniqueness, they can be assured of your self-worth and your qualifications by the fee you expect. Charging well below the going rate often happens because you want to make sure all in need can afford you. This is doing an injustice to all parties involved.

It also reflects a beginner's nervousness.

A colleague spent valuable money, time, and energy completing a strenuous coaching program. When it was time to hang out her shingle, she did so at less than fifty percent of current competitive rates. She forgot that potential clients are attracted by competency and confidence. They can be repulsed by cheap pricing and an attitude of unworthiness. Her feelings of being a newbie betrayed her trained competency.

Next, she felt the need to take courses in business, marketing, and public speaking. Becoming a perpetual student was the mask hiding her insecurities, her fear of being a successful entrepreneur or failing miserably.

Conversely, egoic excess over the industry's norm limits the number of potential clients and weakens your reputation. Instead of experienced and wise, you expose yourself to the criticism of just being in it for the money.

Avoid the extremes.

Research Current Fees

Professional organizations can be helpful in determining what the going rates are in a geographic territory. A going fee in Arkansas is probably different than in New York.

Exercise caution to avoid the appearance of price fixing. Ask around. People are helpful in filling in information needed. Even potential competitors typically will share information about fee structures.

Your Comfort Level

This can be a trap. For the untested entrepreneur, your self-worth is being established. Thus, you see fees set too low. For overtly confident people, fees may be arbitrarily high.

Checking in with your comfort level is wise. Checking with a trusted friend or experienced coach also shows wisdom. You do not know what you don't know.

As a friend of mine says, "You can't see the jar of mayo from inside the jar." A view from outside the jar is always helpful.

Calculate Income Based on Volume

There is only so much clock time and energy available to you each day. It is easy to figure annual income based on fees charged. Do not stop there. Do not get trapped into equating number of hours worked as the sole source of your prosperity.

Your enthusiasm for your work and your ability to be far reaching will come through thinking outside the box. How else do you share your gifts? How else is that revenue generated? Corporations are often amenable to having their name mentioned as a sponsor. Wealthier individuals are often looking for a channel of good in the world they may support.

Revenue may be significantly enhanced by your own creativity and willingness to ask.

Your time is valuable. Your expertise is well-earned. Your love and compassion are well-practiced. People need you, and they are willing to exchange value for your presence in their lives. Knowing the going rate in your industry allows you to marry your remuneration with your own self-worth.

THE VALUE OF YOUR SERVICES

You bring to the table of life your unique combination of business experiences, emotional reactions, fears, ultimate successes, profound learning, personal experiences, and corresponding attitudes. The service you offer may be similar to what others offer, but your uniqueness is unmatchable, unrepeatable, and special.

You are bringing *you* to the relationship and only you can do that. That is so good, I invite you to re-read the previous paragraph.

Know Yourself and Your Motivations

Entrepreneurs, especially burgeoning entrepreneurs, sometimes fall into the trap of letting others determine their worth and their motivations. Being crystal clear about what you want – and why you want it – helps you avoid letting others define you in ways that are unappealing or just outright wrong.

It was a hot, sticky afternoon in Springfield, Ohio, in 1952. I was seven years old and firmly rooted on the front porch of Grandma's apartment house. A bit tired from an afternoon of play, I was almost ready to head inside. We always played outside. There you could see who in the neighborhood was out and about.

The girl's name I have long forgotten. The long, curly, crazy hair I will never forget. The outraged mother I will never forget. My own mother I wanted to forget.

How did that huge mound of double bubble pink gum get out of my mouth? Perhaps devoid of flavor I just yearned to be free of it. My hand bravely rescued it from the saliva-filled dungeon in which it had been worked over. With a majestic sense of freedom, I flung it off the porch straight into the huge mound of messy curly red hair. With an unnecessary scream heard around the then-quiet neighborhood, my friend made a mountain out of a mole hill. "So what?" I thought. "Just pull it out."

The red-haired mother came running. My mother abandoned the kitchen, instantly appearing on that front porch looking confused. It took only seconds for the disgusted and angry little redhead to weave a story of how I didn't really like her and deliberately threw my gum to mess up her beautiful locks.

There were other legitimate claims that could have been made. But both mothers knew the attention needed to be on the immediate problem. There simply was too much gum mangled among the naturally curly long hair to just pull it out. Oh, no, the worst was decided. My playmate screamed bloody murder as the moms took scissors to the damaged hair.

It was over within a minute. So was our friendship. Somehow, I felt relieved. Had I deliberately thrown that gum in her hair?

Clearly, my motivations were called into question and wrongfully decided by the other three people involved. Make sure you understand your own motivations and determine their worth for yourself.

God Qualities

Realizing you are combinations of God qualities and personal shadows allows you to present yourself as an evolving being. But where is your emphasis? Too often the shadow side dominates your self-image and internal conversation. To counter that, regularly review your God qualities. Often these come from feedback from others, as well as your self-knowledge.

I know I am compassionate, altruistic, and generous. I know that instinctively and those qualities are confirmed when acknowledged by others. I know from observing my own behavior over decades of dramatic change that perseverance has dominated my energy, my intentions, and my accomplishments. I find it a trait valued in my core family.

As you read the following childhood experience, see if you can identify the hidden perseverance in each of us. Yes, the shadow side will be all too apparent so see if you can identify the perseverance in the characters.

Raised in a Barn

It was a cold, damp Sunday morning in Ohio. The barn we converted into a home lacked insulation. The wood-burning stove, in what we designated as the kitchen, became a focal point for family activity. We heated our clothes there, got dressed nearby, and generally hung out. I never fully realized how poor we were. Barn or a house, it all felt like home to me.

My oldest brother, affectionately called Dink, put his only pair of dress shoes in the oven and then promptly forgot them. It took very little time for that faithful, hot stove to convert size 12 leather shoes to a curled up, dried out, mangled ball. Oh no!

When Dink remembered where he left his shoes, all hell broke loose. Dad was loudest, ranting about the stupidity of his son. One thing Dad valued was a good pair of men's dress

shoes. They had to be Hanover's, Dad's favor-
ite. Mom appeared devasted as she immedi-
ately retreated into that habit of pondering for
which she was the queen. "How can I get some
money to replace my son's Sunday's shoes?"
she mentally fretted. My brother, Louie, just
observed the drama, so happy it was not one of
his "stupid moves." I felt the same way, relieved
it was Dink on the firing line, not me.

Dink was a senior at Catholic Central High
School and, as such, having one decent pair
of dress shoes was important. The only other
option was the laced-up pair of work shoes he
wore on the wrecking jobs he worked. Thus, he
donned the work shoes, hoping no one would
notice. Everyone did.

I quietly accompanied the family to St. Joe's
for Mass, praying for peace at home and that
somehow Mom would be able to find the money
for new shoes.

Perseverance is a God quality to be nourished. Did you notice the level of perseverance within each of the characters?

The value of your services will be dramatically affected by your God qualities. What are they and how do they manifest in your world?

I AM THAT, I AM

I modified this iconic scriptural line, as I'm sure you noticed. Normally we say, *"I Am That I Am,"* and then ponder its meaning. Here I invite you to take the list of God qualities you, and others see in you, then say, *"I Am That* (speaking your God quality list)." Complete your affirmation by finishing with, *"I Am."*

Here is an example. *"I Am That* [compassionate, generous, prosperous, spiritual, smart person]. *I Am!"*

This iconic saying becomes a powerful affirmation for your own goodness. *"I Am That, I Am!"* One comma makes a profound difference.

Namaste in Action

Understanding the values and gifts you bring to your clients is powerful. Simultaneously, seeing the good in them and praising it has often changed the direction of a person's life.

You are engaged in this career shift, so you can continue making a significant difference for those attracted to your services. Seeing the God qualities in your clients is the greatest gift you can give them. For this, you can expect to be indispensable, joyous, and well compensated.

A Willing Recipient of Good

Strike a balance between your desire to be of service and the legitimate recognition of your wisdom. Then you get to exhale. You will know intuitively as well as from your income flow and full calendar. That lucrative, yet fair representation of abundance is yours to enthusiastically expect and legitimately enjoy.

Consider my experience of providing a flow of good, and the remarkable consequences, as I exercised a desire to be of service. As a CFP I provided a special-client-theme annually. It was a related yet outside-the-box experience for my clients.

I met a female court reporter and husband videographer who relished their side business of making video recordings of the elderly. I offered their services to record my client's older relatives. Armed with the court reporting and camera equipment they were unattached and thus fearless in their ability to ask questions.

Two stories linger as special. The court reporter asked a Grandmother, "Do you remember your first kiss?" She lit up, sharing the story of her first love, whom she married, sent to war two days later, and by whom she became a widow two weeks later. When the gifted video was viewed, family members were shocked there was a man in Grandma's life before their grandfather. No one had ever asked about her first kiss.

One of the grandfathers was asked, "From your life experiences, what are you most proud of?" They anticipated him declaring his grandchildren, the kids, his long marriage, his career, etc. His response was the Medal of Honor given for his valor in saving many comrades in a momentous battle. When this gifted video was viewed, family members vaguely recalled they thought Grandpa had served but he never spoke of those years and no one asked. They were shocked that what he viewed as the most important thing in his life had never been shared.

The lucrative flow of my earned abundance allowed me to provide this experience for my clients. As you develop your own corporation or LLC, stay conscious of how you can give back to those who trust and choose to do business with you.

PAY ATTENTION TO THE FINE PRINT

Exceptions—Pro Bono Clients

Most people in the personal growth and self-help arenas have clients who expect service for free. Exercise compassion, realizing their attitude of abundance is still expanding. Be creative with that potential client by asking them what remuneration would look like.

Asking them may be their greatest call to growth. It puts the issue of value back in their court. One of my favorite cards from my Notes to Self, published each Friday, is *Price is an issue only in the absence of value.*

The overall attitude that spiritual services of counseling, coaching, and advising should be done for free is a dynamic to be avoided. It flies in the face of the Law of Circulation and proliferates usury. Do not go there. We teach by everything we say and do, so watch what you are teaching.

If your potential client is experiencing financial hardship, and your services are helpful, allow that client to suggest other ways they might remunerate you. That is both compassionate and creative. Having an account for tuition assistance available to those unable to pay for your professional services is often a win/win for everyone.

Professional Trades

Often an exchange of services is of paramount importance. It may be valuable networking, exposing you to referable services. As a legitimate form of remuneration, it still should be minimal. Your mortgage and groceries cannot be handled with the currency of exchanged services or networking opportunities.

If you choose to engage in a trade, be sure to document what each party will provide in detail. Include the services, time, and other variables so each side will feel the trade is fair. Also be sure to include a timeframe, so the trade is limited in scope and has a firm end date.

Frequently in trading services, one party believes they have given more than they have received. This can lead to disagreements and long-term damage to both reputations. If you suspect this might be the case, avoid the trade altogether.

Being firm and fair, making all decisions transparent, and knowing when the trade agreement ends can help avoid a long-term bad result for everyone involved.

Packaging Your Services

People of all economic status love a legitimate bargain. Packages provide an indirect level of commitment, affords you up front revenue, and your clients enjoy a percentage break.

Give your stand-alone fee first. Clients can use that watermark to judge the value of a package of three, five, or more.

POINTS TO PONDER/QUESTIONS TO JOURNAL

1. Is your remuneration in concert with your talent and services?

2. What research have you done of your industry to determine the range of compensation? Where do you fall within this range?

3. How does your self-image affect your remuneration expectations? How do you think others judge you: ego driven or quietly shy?

4. Outside of hours in a workday, how else can your services be judged as

contributing? If a potential client asked, "What's in it for me?," how would you explain?

5. What are your God qualities? How do you allow them to manifest?

CHAPTER FIVE

Seeing the Bigger Picture

If one is lucky, a solitary fantasy can totally transform one million realities.
—Maya Angelou

LEARN SOMETHING NEW

Embrace New Experiences

You are an entrepreneur because you have big ideas and you want to bring them to fruition. My sense is that at more than one point in your life, you had an experience where you just knew this to be true. It may have been a dream, or an experience and you just felt it at the core of your being.

Successful entrepreneurs embrace new experiences, including measuring themselves against the larger culture to see where they fit and whether they can adapt.

It was a lovely fall day with crisp air mingling with the late afternoon gentle sun. Working as cashier at Wilson's House of Leather and Suede, I had a perfect view of 16th Street traffic. I loved downtown Denver.

A beautiful stretch white limo pulled up. I waited with bated breath for the occupant to emerge. When he did, I fell in love. At least 6'6", this thin, muscular, royal gentleman owned the street. He slowly glanced in all four directions before regally heading for our front door.

My heart stopped as I stared at his Kennedy-style chiseled chin, handsomely protected by the pure white hat and flanked by the entire white costume: white shirt, tie, and vest under an exquisite white suit, draped by a full-length white coat, pointing down to his white socks and shoes. Whoa! As he entered the store, he flashed a smile that handsomely displayed the diamond embedded in his front tooth.

Immediately the store manager, Mrs. Trujillo, was at his side. A warm embrace clearly indicated this is a regular client for whom she had great regard. Duh. Of course. His visits probably made her sales quota for a month.

While they chatted, I became obsessed observing young women as they slipped into his royal carriage, that elegant white stretch limo. "Trespassing," I thought. I wanted to let him know but intuitively knew not to. The nervous sales assistant and our economically pleased Mrs. Trujillo hurried the 12 full-length, leather, elegant coats out to the ladies waiting in the limo.

As the cashier, I was impressed by my first experience of seeing a huge wad of hundred-dollar bills emerge casually from someone's person. His calm demeanor soothed me as I shook in a maze of distraction. I was so grateful for Mrs. Trujillo at the register, as I lost all ability to calculate 12 tags.

Aware my hand was shaking, I extended his change in cash. It afforded me a moment in time that literally stood still. I was transfixed on the diamond-studded tooth as he flashed a delicious smile and with a wave of his arm declared, "That's yours." I stopped breathing.

I remained transfixed as the limo drove slowly away. It was years later I learned this beautiful man was a well know character in the story of Denver's iconic citizens.

Imagine this former nun, shielded as I had been from many of the world's realities, finding that I could accept and affirm those with whom I seemed to have nothing in common. This moment in time proved to me I could not only exist in the broader culture of the time, I could accept and thrive among people I never dreamed I would encounter.

VISIONING

Strengthening our ability to grasp the bigger picture, no matter our preferred style of interacting, is available through the dynamic technique of visioning. This exercise allows the experience of what has been described as channeling divine ideas. Thus, we create an inspired framework around the issue at hand.

Visioning is both simple as a process and rich in its results. Here is the recipe.

The venue is you alone or, better yet, with

a small group of trusted friends. Two to five is excellent. Present the topic. It could be insights into starting your small business. It could be insights into building a team of support people. It could be insights into prosperity for your family. It can be any issue for which you desire guidance.

You now declare an openness for all present to channel, to be conduits for the universe's ideas. To facilitate that flow of intuitive richness, you ask a series of questions. Quiet time is allowed while attendees record their reactions. These may demonstrate in words, pictures, colors, feelings, etc. All insights are welcomed and recorded.

Questions follow this general format:

1. What is in the **highest and best interest** regarding me starting my own business... [restate the vision in your own words].

    As ideas come, participants record those insights in their notebooks. When the group is ready, proceed in silence.

2. What do I need to **embrace** for the realization of the vision? Repeat the recording process.

3. What do I need to **release** for the realization of the vision? Repeat the recording process.

4. Is there **anything else** choosing to present itself regarding this vision? Repeat the recording process.

Everyone shares their insights aloud for the first question. Patterns may emerge, be recognized, and discussed. The modality of sharing and looking for patterns on each question is completed.

Herein lies the richness for the participants as they discuss their insights and reactions to this adventure. An ending discussion further enriches the participants when the coordinator asks, "How was this exercise for you?" Often, they too are motivated to form their own group to vision for an issue of theirs.

The results of a visioning exercise are typically twofold, gratitude for the participants and fodder for future insightful experiences.

My God and I Are One

Fundamental to superb visioning is being grounded in oneness with Spirit. This awareness eliminates the exercise from becoming brainstorming, which solely engages our human mind. Visioning is a vehicle by which Spirit moves through us as channels. This is co-creation at its best.

Visioning also reinforces awareness of oneness with each other. Inviting others to vision with and for your entrepreneur venture is a mutually beneficial gift. You are acknowledging your trust in their ability to channel divine ideas and the participants are acknowledging you by carving out the time to support your vision.

This is Namaste at its best. The God in me recognizes and loves the God in you.

Embrace Your Divine Channeling

Here we allow our ego to take a rest. Trust that no one is judging whether your download is meaty, meaningful, or creative. No color, feeling, energy, word, or picture is irrelevant. Patterns linking the seemingly diverse sensations often reveal precious insights.

Exercising your intuitive abilities enhances

your insights. You get to trust as you allow it to flow. You get to trust that the deeper meaning may not be apparent until sometime in the future. You get to trust the wisdom of the host to blend and elicit richness from everything that is shared.

Flowing Without Judgments

When visioning in a group, you may find yourself wanting to make a significant contribution. Thus, a sense of judging your insights anchors itself in the process. This is not helpful. Gently ask the ego to step down, for Spirit to dominate, and for yourself to trust your intuition. That is a powerful formula for directing this energy.

I am privileged when asked to participate in a visioning session. Frequency increases expertise and familiarity. It is a vehicle of contribution, compassion, and gifting. I often will vision alone with my journal. That allows practicing the art of channeling while the current topic from my life is enriched by my insights.

LET YOUR DREAM UNFOLD

Details

At times, the daily activities involved in unfolding your dream can fully use your time and energy. Being mired down in detail is a trap well worth avoiding. Yet, details are crucial.

Different personalities experience different strengths relating to the world. For example, those who are people oriented, visionary, or structure bound do not always see the value of details. Some find details irritating. Yet their value is immeasurable.

I want the pilot of my plane to be incredibly detail oriented, especially during the preflight check. I want the surgeon who put in my new hip to be exceptionally detail oriented. I want my CPA to live in the world of important details.

Importance of Self-Diagnostic Assessment Tools

Focusing on your strengths and avoiding your weaker areas is what most successful coaches do. It is imperative that coaches know their players well.

As an entrepreneur, you are both the coach and the primary player. Knowing yourself while acting as your own coach is challenging. An objective assessment is invaluable.

There are numerous well-established tools available. Take as many as you are called to and patterns. I have invested in and enjoyed over a dozen and found them all valuable.

Understanding Leads to Respect

You see this in every aspect of your life: in politics, religion, business and families. When you do not walk a mile on the other person's path, you easily become void of that fundamental respect, the glue that binds people and nations.

Beginning with understanding your own strengths and shadows expands your ability to experience that rare gift of compassion for others.

Go with Your Strengths

Once grounded in your self-assessments, explore how your strengths serve you now. Starting a new career may need strengths you have yet to develop. Meanwhile, for those skill sets lacking, you can hire the work done. Do what you are good at and what you love.

Volunteers, family, friends, and employees can be found with skills you lack. This is done by becoming selective about how you filter your energies. Yes, most entrepreneurs end up being the person wearing many hats for which many skills are required. As you progress, heighten your awareness of your strengths, move toward the activities demanding those traits and begin strategizing how you might have others deal with the rest.

REFLECTIONS

So many desire to be co-creators with the Divine. You want access to insights that are powerful beyond words. You want to make a profound difference in the world. You want your time on planet Earth to mean something, nay, to mean a great deal. You want to live a life of prosperity and to be happy. You wonder how.

The art of visioning and all that entails is a powerful tool assisting us in this quest. Consider this real-world experience of mine.

What do you do when you are broke at thirty-three and need to start life all over again from scratch? It would take some unusual circumstances for this to occur. For me it unfolded when I chose to leave my life as a teaching Catholic Sister.

The Sisters of Charity returned to the exiting nuns the hundred-dollar dowry originally brought to the community on entrance day. What a godsend that was to me.

Taking my returned dowry, I headed to Colfax Ave, one of the more colorful streets in downtown Denver. The Goodwill store was loaded in a sporadic, unorganized kind of crazy way. I knew I needed some lay clothes and kitchen supplies, so I headed to the piles of jeans and chose my first pair. Feeling a need for a casual outfit of comfort, I stumbled upon a rack of men's white shirts with long tails, the perfect style to hide burgeoning wide thighs. This was a perfect outfit for weekends.

Kitchen supplies held their own area of display every bit as chaotic as the rest of the store. Rumbling through donated used dishes, I found a set of red plastic tumblers, perfect water glasses. I had to disregard consistency of design as I put together a set of twelve knives, forks, and spoons.

Calculating several other needed items, such as a few pots and a small skillet, I knew I was making a significant dent in my hundred-dollar limit. I cared. I wanted a little change for some unknown reason. Perhaps it was ego, as I surely did not want to get to *the checkout counter and put something back because I did not have the money. How embarrassing. Really, for a 33-year-old woman with a master's degree in education, that would be too humiliating.*

There was great joy in this shopping spree because I got to choose. It was a rite of passage away from the vow of poverty to the independence of self-choice. Although in my early thirties, I still felt like I was eighteen, leaving home and starting out on an adult path that was more than welcomed.

Valuable life lessons were acted out that day. Staying within a budget, purchasing needed items first, and spending less money than I had, evidenced superior habits of money management.

POINTS TO PONDER/QUESTIONS TO JOURNAL

1. Gather a group of people whose insights you admire and trust. Engage them in a visioning exercise for your success as an entrepreneur, the success of your endeavor, or any topic for which you would like insights.

2. Be willing to be on a Visioning Team for others, not only to serve but to practice your channeling skills as well.

3. Prioritize the practical results from your visioning session and act on the ones you see have immediate merit.

4. Focusing on your strengths and designing your job description accordingly begins with knowing your strengths. What are yours and how can your daily activities be based on them?

5. Understanding means to stand under, which means to look up to. Who in your life deserves greater respect? How might you demonstrate that now?

CHAPTER SIX

A Life Transformed

"Live Simply So Others May Simply Live"
—Elizabeth Bayley Seton

I AM INSPIRED by anyone, and especially women, who live their lives outside the box. They exude the qualities of successful entrepreneurship. Such is the iconic American woman who exemplified entrepreneurism and lived a life of inspiration for generations.

As you enjoy her remarkable story, notice the skills you may wish to emulate as a successful entrepreneur. Immerse yourself in the life of

Elizabeth Bayley Seton. She did not just think outside the box, *she lived out there.*

If interviewed today, Elizabeth would likely tell us, "I was born in 1774 and only enjoyed the presence of my mother for three years. I have no memory of her. My stepmother was openly resistant to me. As a teen I fell in love with a handsome man and together we bore and began raising five beautiful children, my 'darlings' as I called them. William, my beloved husband, lost his father, causing his six younger siblings to join our family."

This came at a time when the Setons were socially prominent in New York, as evidenced by their membership in the fashionable lower Manhattan's Trinity Episcopal Church. There Elizabeth was involved in the founding of the Society for the Relief of Poor Widows with Small Children.

Here is a valuable insight from today's archivist and historian, Sister Judith Metz, S.C. "The Society required them to handle tasks previously performed only by men, negotiating with government officials, interacting with the society at large, and learning to be good managers. They learned to face opposition and ridicule, as noted by founder Isabella Graham who described the Society as 'feeble in its origin, the jest of most, the ridicule of many,' particularly 'the men [who] could not allow our sex the steadiness and perseverance necessary to establish such an undertaking.' These women maneuvered through political channels to gain the support they needed, learning in the process how to be savvy negotiators. They incorporated their organization so that they could legally own property, utilized their right of petition for public money, and engaged in fundraising activities.

"Women of the gentry responded overwhelmingly to this new initiative, bringing with them their personal experiences, religious beliefs, educational skills, and financial resources that shaped the Society. By the time of the first official meeting of the organization, two hundred and fourteen had subscribed as members, at three dollars per year. By the end of their first year in operation the women had one hundred and fifty-two widows with four hundred and twenty children younger than twelve on their relief books and continued with similar numbers in subsequent years.

"Elizabeth took on responsibility as a

manager of the Society in 1802 and served as treasurer in 1803. As one of twelve managers, she was responsible for the distribution of relief in a designated section of the city. She visited the homes of poor women to evaluate their character and circumstances to determine if they were eligible for assistance."

Elizabeth's beloved, William Magee Seton, was also a successful entrepreneur involved in the shipping industry until disasters struck. There was no insurance coverage available to protect the cargo, so each storm, raid of pirates, or fire cost her beloved dearly. During their monetary crisis, Elizabeth assisted him by managing the firm's accounting. Circumstances continued and the company went bankrupt in 1801.

It is said that Elizabeth was often quoted as saying, "Live simply so that others may simply live." Losing all their possessions, including the family home in lower Manhattan, was their lived reality as William began to show signs of tuberculosis.

William had visited important counting houses in Europe, becoming a special friend of Filippo Filicchi, a renowned merchant of Livorno, Italy. William, Elizabeth, and their oldest daughter, Anna Maria, sailed to the warm climate of Italy, praying the climate would restore his health.

They anticipated being the houseguests of the Filicchi family. However, authorities feared yellow fever and quarantined the family within a stone lazaretto. The Filicchi family advocated for them during their month of seclusion. Yet it was only two weeks after their release that William died. Elizabeth was left a widow with young children at age twenty-nine.

While living with the Filicchi family, Elizabeth relished her quiet time in the simplicity of their home chapel. "When so rich a harvest is before us, why do we not gather it?" she asked. "All is in our hands if we will but use it." This is a powerfully positive attitude amid despair.

And use it she did. Elizabeth developed a fierce devotion to the Eucharist. Deeply moved, she ultimately converted to Roman Catholicism. On her return to New York, she rightly feared the ostracism from the elite social and economically prosperous groups who would not allow a Catholic in their midst.

These initial years were marked by disappointments and failures. Rampant anti-Catholic prejudice prevented her from beginning a school and challenged her ability to provide for her children. Thus, she made the tough decision to leave New York.

The newly widowed Mrs. Seton ultimately arrived in Baltimore and was invited to be a school mistress. Eventually, Samuel Sutherland Cooper, a wealthy seminarian, purchased two hundred and sixty-nine acres near Emmitsburg for the establishment of a school for girls, care for the elderly, and development of job skills. Elizabeth played a pivotal role in the creation as director of this educational institution.

This seemingly insurmountable challenge must have been causative for one of her iconic quotes, "Cheerfulness prepares a glorious mind for all the noblest acts."

The noble act was opening St. Joseph's Free School for needy girls. Again, this was Elizabeth living outside the box as she formed America's first Catholic school. She staffed this educational institution with what became Catholic sisters, women attracted to the religious lifestyle perpetuated by Elizabeth.

Sister Judith Metz richly adds, "The story of the conversion of a woman of her birth and social standing became widely disseminated among the small numbers of Catholics throughout the country. Thus, her activities gained attention and soon priests began recommending young women to join her.

"At the same time she dealt with priest superiors who were often at a distance and sometimes had ideas contrary to her own. Nevertheless, she found ways to exert her will when their clerical demands interfered with her plans. She negotiated property dealings and arranged for legal incorporation, as well as overseeing building projects and the opening of new works in faraway cities. The success and permanence of the works she established are testimony to the solid foundation on which they were built."

Smartly, St. Joseph's Academy welcomed the addition of boarding students who paid tuition. This way the newly formed Sisters of Charity were able to subsidize their charitable mission of educating impoverished girls. In her journal she declared, "Divine Providence guided me and our little community through the poverty and unsettling first years." Like a true entrepreneur, Elizabeth grew in clarity about her mission and pressed on with all the practical skills necessary for success.

During that time, numerous women joined the Sisters of Charity. Elizabeth pronounced her vows of poverty, chastity, and obedience and was called Mother Seton. The historic numbers indicated her success. Between 1809-1820, ninety-eight candidates enlisted and eighty-six joined the new community, seventy percent of whom remained Sisters of Charity for life.

Today, six orders of religious women trace their origins to Mother Seton. After a short but stellar life, Mother Elizabeth Ann Seton succumbed to tuberculosis at age 46.

James Gibbons, archbishop of Baltimore, initiated her cause for canonization in 1882. It was not officially introduced at the Vatican until 1940. There it made steady progress. John XXIII declared Elizabeth venerable in 1959, beatifying her in 1963. Pope Paul VI canonized Saint Elizabeth Ann Seton on September 14, 1975.

During her extraordinary life she exemplified the skills and courage of a true entrepreneur. Things change. Her path included a difficult childhood, being a New York socialite, declaring bankruptcy, being a devoted wife, the mother of five children, stepmother to an additional six, surviving as a displaced widow, bravely converting to Roman Catholicism, founding the Sisters of Charity, while working as a tireless educator, social minister, and a spiritual leader. Whoa!

Finding her legacy still outside the box, Elizabeth Bayley Seton, the wealthy, widowed, Protestant mother of five, is recognized as the founder of the American Catholic School System, the first ecclesiastical Mother of a truly American-based religious order and the first citizen-born American saint.

Elizabeth focused her extraordinary leadership locally. Inadvertently, she set the stage for worldwide influence. Elizabeth Bayley Seton was among those in the Federalist period who opened new horizons for women in the public arena. Nineteenth and twentieth century women's reform and feminist organizations moved far beyond what early benevolent societies envisioned or accomplished for women, but they stood on the shoulders of these first female giants.

What changes are you willing to undergo to become the entrepreneur you are called to be in your industry? Sometimes greatness is thrust upon us, and at other times we deliberately choose it. Choose wisely.

I celebrate you being willing to weigh carefully all the aspects we covered in this deep dive of success and spirituality, for what you do is important. Your prosperity is important. Your ability to experience the fullness of joy is important.

The journey continues!

POINTS TO PONDER/QUESTIONS TO JOURNAL

1. How have you already experienced being "outside the box."? What was it like and what gift was in it for you?

2. How does Elizabeth Seton's iconic saying, "Live simply so that others may simply live," serve you in your entrepreneurial quest? What could that mean for you?

3. Elizabeth learned to pay attention to and manage finances even while her heart energy was elsewhere. Are you willing to do what it takes to create the prosperity desired? How might that look for you?

4. Elizabeth's entrepreneurial success was

challenged by the prejudice of religious intolerance and being a single woman. Have you experienced prejudicial barriers and how did you handle them?

5. What in Elizabeth Seton's life touched you most profoundly? How can her trust in the Universe, focus on details, and sheer determinism support your entrepreneurial venture?

INSPIRATIONAL IDEAS
TO ACT ON NOW